THE LAST MILKWEED

An Autumnal Anthology of Poetry

TUPELO PRESS

NORTH ADAMS, MA

The Last Milkweed: An Autumnal Anthology of Poetry
Introductions and compilation copyright © 2025 Tupelo Press. All rights reserved.

Edited by: Alan Berolzheimer, Jeffrey Levine, & Allison O'Keefe

Library of Congress Cataloging-in-Publication data available upon request.
ISBN-13: 978-1-961209-25-1

Cover and text design by Allison O'Keefe
Cover photo by Jeffrey Levine

Photography Copyright © Jeffrey Levine

First paperback edition February 2025

Tupelo Press
P.O. Box 1767
North Adams, Massachusetts 01247
(413) 664-9611 / Fax: (413) 664-9711
editor@tupelopress.org / www.tupelopress.org

Tupelo Press is an award-winning independent literary press that publishes fine fiction, non-fiction, and poetry in books that are a joy to hold as well as read. Tupelo Press is a registered 501(c)(3) nonprofit organization, and we rely on public support to carry out our mission of publishing extraordinary work that may be outside the realm of the large commercial publishers. Financial donations are welcome and are tax deductible.

CONTENTS

Preface: On Autumn and the Unsayable   vii

Elise Paschen
    Sumac in Pawhuska   3
Bonney Hartley
    Ordaining the Ordinary   5
Martha Ronk
    Queen Anne's Lace   6
    October Weed   8
Didi Jackson
    Open   10
rose auslander
    Pack your old summers in boxes   12
    As the weather turns   15
Eva Hooker
    Like the Wild Thyme, Unseen Dry Salvages   16
James McCorkle
    Red Knot   19
Mackenzie Schubert Polonyi Donnelly
    Estefelé / Toward Evening   21
    Dear Aceso   24
Maija Rhee Devine
    Autumn   27
s. d. lishan
    October 23   29
Christopher Buckley
    Agnostic   31
Cynthia Bargar
    Atonement after Sunset at Ponyhenge   36

Arthur Solway
    Mid-Autumn Diary   39
Gillian Cummings
    As Sleep Comes   40
Becka Mara McKay
    The Judgment of the Open Pit *(Exodus 21:23)*   42
William Orem
    The Festal Letters   45
William Barnes
    the art of collage   47
Brenda Beardsley
    troglodyte   50
Kristina Erny
    Shuttle   53
Michael Chitwood
    Falling Leaves Catching in Fallen Leaves   54
Deborah Gorlin
    Aging in Place   57
Annette Sisson
    At sixteen, instead of practicing piano   59
Karen Earle
    [dew-starred]   61
Laura Budofsky Wisniewski
    Math Sonnet #1   63
    When the Leaves Have Fallen, the Zen Master Stops Eating   64
Marjorie Maddox
    Midlife Mowing   66
Jenny Grassl
    Earth Sings Greensleeves to Mankind   69
Susan McCabe
    Ovid Speaks to Bark, in These Times of Our Sickness   70

Katherine Cota Macdonald
    Sundust   72

Sarah Maclay
    Swansong ~ Autumn Aubade   75

Luisa A. Igloria
    The Myth of Distance   78

John James
    The Field Which Had Been A Meadow Once   80

Alicia Rebecca Myers
    Loss   82

Rosemary Herbert
    In Elsie's Garden   84

Libby Maxey
    The New Actaeon   85

L. Stuart
    Autumn Understory   87

Jon Davis
    Wallace Stevens in the Blackfoot River Valley   88

Gibson Fay-LeBlanc
    From Room to Room   91

Veronica Patterson
    Autumn Is a Honey Locust Tree   93

Calleja Smiley Welsh
    The tree and I have nothing   95

Mara Adamitz Scrupe
    Lawrence Campground Windfall Orchard   97

Natalie Taylor
    Shouldering into Rest   101

Steven Salmoni
    Landscape, with Changing Weather   103

Rebecca A. Durham
    Wood Parade   107
Lisa Furmanski
    primer of prairie portent   109
Preeti Parikh
    The [   ] of Form   111
Rick Hilles
    Prayer for This Morning   115
G. C. Waldrep
    Autumn Celebrant   118
    Resting Crown   121
    Milkweed Remnant, Colton Point Road   123

Contributors   127

ON AUTUMN AND THE UNSAYABLE,
A PREFACE TO *THE LAST MILKWEED*

In writing inspired by the autumnal (in all of its exterior and interior manifestations) we find a world of difference between trying to capture the unsayable through mere description—or indulgence in plangent abstractions—and forging a bodily connection with what originally brought us into the moment of the poem.

The same goes for simply "describing" what we see. If poetry merely took on the role of description, we'd all be writing catalog copy. Contributors were asked to provide work that moves beyond descriptions of milkweed or falling leaves, that transcends the notion that the "autumnal" is about foliage or plummeting temperatures. Sure, autumn can be found both in things and in ideas, but those are only surface layers.

We want readers to feel something unaccountable. How might that happen? As ever, poems take root in the soil of mystery. From that beginning, the success of a poem is all about the choices we make, and the risks we take in making them. We form our world out of what we choose to see. So much the better if those choices arise out of our unconscious selves, leaving the rational, waking self behind, as we do in dreams.

Remembering that the poem's suspended moment ("a momentary stay against confusion," says Robert Frost) is a threshold between disorder and order can tell us so much about poetry and about ourselves. The dictionary definition of threshold is "the sill of a doorway," "the entrance to a house or building" and, in psychology and physiology, "the point where a stimulus is of sufficient intensity to produce an effect." That effect embodies a sudden awareness of the disorder—that moment when we and our poem feel destabilized—and the imagination's response to it.

It can be helpful to go directly to the most physical manifestations. Imagine the doorsill as both entrance to and exit from a house. A threshold, then, a place of transition. That liminal location where a person—or a poet— might pause to give form to the inner. According to Marie Howe, poetry is "a cup of language to hold what can't be said . . . Every poem holds the unspeakable inside it. The unsayable." What can't be said. That's what we are compelled to write about, and how we are compelled to write it.

In other words, the work of the poem is to help both writer and reader come to know something beyond what we already knew, or thought we knew. In *A Lover's Discourse*, Roland Barthes writes: "Language is a skin. I rub my language against the other. It is as if I had words instead of fingers, or fingers at the tip of my words."

We have asked our contributors to permit their language to become their skin. To let their language rub up against any part or parts of the autumnal world that calls to them, whether from the outside in, or the inside out.

In other words, these autumn poems need not be about, or even mention fallen leaves, or milkweed, or even "autumn." Autumn is the inspiration, but not necessarily the destination. The destination is, as ever, discovery.

Jeffrey Levine

THE LAST MILKWEED

An Autumnal Anthology of Poetry

Elise Paschen

Sumac in Pawhuska

ákahamı žúuce dée, pée duuštáke hta de?
Who is going to undress that one with the red coat?
— from the *Osage Dictionary* by Carolyn Quintero

Against black jacks,
                    the wedding coat
                                        red of sumac

flares bright, soon
                    to be stripped
                                        bare. The tires

drum a trot
                    rhythm through
                                        the tall-grass prairie,

a horse-raiding
                    song, centuries old.
                                        Dried-up stalks,

ghosts of sunflowers,
                    bow down in fields.
                                        During the Drum

Ceremony, a wife
                    will bestow her wedding
                                        coat, the one handed

down through her family,
                    once a soldier's. What
                                        can I release

from this mortal heart?
                    A red-tailed hawk
                                        alights in a cedar.

Come wildfire
                    season, those trees
                                        will explode.

Bonney Hartley

Ordaining the Ordinary

Kneel down / Mud seeps
Lost legends / Smoke offering
Beetle's bite / Merciful leaves
Curled crisply / Faraway train

Decayed layer / Cake sliced thickly
Look up a bit / Pregnant milkweed
Seeds clasping / Prickled pod
Plumped cheeks / Baby, I love your sigh

Hair tufts gleam / Mother's hum
Constant listener / Auntie River at rest
Two ducks backward / Reluctant novices
Spine of bent grasses / Chapped fingers smear

Colonies underground / Tiny drumbeats remember
Melody of their bones / Feeding you
Blue icicles pierce / Porcupine path
Pulse of bittersweet / Color down the drain

She knows medicine / Spice cabinets
No expectation / Sumac's flame
Signal on dry branch / Suppress the sneeze
Surrender season / Sun lowers lantern

Can you repeat / Pitch of prayer / Once said here
Stand back up / Time for soup / Relatives assemble
Always surrounded / A million voices / On the land
It quivers / Your breath / The truth of these thighs
Don't crumple / Unfurl / Behold the invitation
To break / To sing / To ignite

Martha Ronk

Queen Anne's Lace

touched once at the center
left alone to lace itself in round-about fringes
left alone at the side of the lockdown fences
at the side of the truckwheel flattened for weeks
left in front of the house with rusted others,
each arm bends in response, a little lean to the left
it scatters itself everywhere east coast west coast
needing only neglect to thrive and memories
of when you first told me of the drop of blood
on her lacemaking, a woman pricked

Martha Ronk

October Weed

twangy, wispy, stick-like on the way to the end
of the road so metaphoric but then it turns a corner
looping around to where the school bus once stopped
these ragged ones clinging to wire fences keeping
chickens in and us out, they blow over so often it's a wonder
and they are what is, like daily life repeated in its round
of dishes, dirty clothes, small irritations erupting
like flowers hanging on for dear life at the far end
of a frail twig and he says you need to appreciate
your life but I hear it best from the weedy thing
that comes up, dots the driveway, blooms

Didi Jackson

Open

The webbing of bare branches
        beneath the chalky sky

spreads like the fan vaulting of a gothic cathedral,
        the old maple now a landmark of our yard.

See how she de-robes each autumn,
        the shine of her bark glistening

in the late hour's rain,
        the dense skirt of bright orange

gathered at her base. And the sun,
        a fallen laundress, gradually washes

away all the colors of the day
        until only the silhouettes

of crown and spark remain.
        Today, a hummingbird

at a cold paltry feeder, its throat
        a slice of sunset, here and now,

defying the laws nature provides.
        Its accomplice: the humid weather

and lack of frost. These warm days
        confuse so many more than just myself.

Aside from the cardinal points
   spinning as if in a washing machine,

I am happy for the late warmth
   that keeps my geraniums in bloom.

A new guilt to take to church, I suppose.
   Even the wind calms after beating

its dry head against our gate,
   lifting the blood-red berries

of the honeysuckle one by one
   to beak after beak after open beak.

rose auslander

Pack your old summers in boxes

if you stay here, it never will change will it, the sea, purling into sand, unraveling from itself & back again, piling itself up on itself & breaking over & over, doing what it does, the breaking, the not being broken, letting you do what you do, the wading in & in to where it will flash freeze you, carry you, spit you out again & again & leave you

buried under cold, wet sand until it doesn't bother you anymore   does it
putting your arms around
the sleeping sun & the cold blue moon
& waiting for night to come.

rose auslander

As the weather turns

it never helps, but sure, wave as they go
beers in hand, skin peeling from the sun, driving
back to everywhere, yelling *Get a car*.
Maybe slow, too slow, here we stay, the rest
of us, gulls, geese, swans, hawks, waves,
the rainy days we walk to work past Kalmus
the weeks the tide neglects to rise
the nights we drink & dig for coins, why not?
As if it matters what we do
the hours we sit, eyes closed, too tired to talk,
those dreams that float & float & float
the times we drop our arms & just stand still
in rushing waves, indifferent sand,
the ice cream melts so fast & then it's winter.

Eva Hooker

Like the Wild Thyme, Unseen
Dry Salvages

The salt is on the briar rose,
The fog is in the fir trees.
—T. S. Eliot

We went out to see the rocks. His "granite teeth" in Gloucester Bay.
We stood silently on Old Garden Beach, scanning the sea.

Giant bushes of white daisy, its frontage.
Purple aster. We scanned the surface as if our eyes could touch
the water—like braille—and read its hand, its starfish, its crabs,
the whale's backbone, the romping seals.

What we found, only tossed-up pieces
of stuff, the guttural croak of a bird, whose kind we do not know.
Northern gannet.

Yet here, where we fail to see what we came
to see, instead, a curved sliver of red and blue and gold. Light
that murmurs. Sea mark we are given.

No salt. No fog.

James McCorkle

Red Knot

Having spent the season to prepare to leave, then going
the night a state of flight, the whole body given to movement—

to the outermost, furthest shore, *playero ártico*—

leaves stain sidewalks with rust-red handprints after a rain, a wind came up
during the night and toppled a dead hawthorn, pulling down a fence—

red-dancing figures, rust pigment blown onto rock faces in sea caves
along Norway's crenellated coast,
dance to sun-cast in *Bardo*, migrant through cave-darknesses—

king on the shore, counting his birds, sitting on his throne, counting
the flocks, red and delicious, on the tide, the red flow, red, king counting in the cold—

the roots rotted away after days of heavy rain, morning lawns a sheen of white frost—

the crossing over, the sentence of light in that migration, one state
to the next, the fall folding after into ground-tightened
days before the snows—

what changes, as in the red knot
in its eighteen thousand miles shrinks gizzard, liver, stomach, and leg muscles,
growing heart and flight muscles and body fat to stay in continuous flight
touching down in Delaware bays for translucent eggs of horseshoe crabs
glistening in black mud, accordions of discs, fatty solar systems necessary
to gorge and then lift into the need to continue—

brown-shovel-shelled, their copper-blue blood, litmus for pathogens, a bay's
no-kill harvest leaves so little left for others—

red knots lift, over sandbars, breakers—

how do I know who I am today—

moving through these states of darkness
as in *the taking care of* or *the providing of*, the dropping away
of one thought after another leaves behind *that*,
but even that ebbs so that all the soul is moves
on, a remnant song, a long swing between the poles—

Mackenzie Schubert Polonyi Donnelly

Estefelé / Toward Evening

Estefelé / Toward Evening

you un-become in becoming autumnal. You relinquish aromatic remembrance
after aromatic remembrance. You relinquish onion, marjoram, mulberry wine.
You relinquish caraway, cauldron of copper or clay, name after name
Even The Anna Grove Old Oak of Szarvas,   even mine.

O tousled meanwhile of anonymity wherein you glisten like a candle-kissed bloodhound—
Here are my syllabic handkerchiefs gold-blossoming almost-apparitional
scents of citrus. Relocate our relation for I am bereft of you. Won't you unscatter
your narrative from untraceable directions & harmonica yourself back?

Emlékek / Remembrances

tearing wind like undisciplined silverware. Be gravitational
with the sacred magnitude of a kitchen. I did not dare ask: what if
amid winter solstice occurs a solar eclipse & you are gone? What then?
I did not dare ask: where am I to find a furnace? (Ours once stoked itself).

O vertebral hearth broom O pulmonic bellows This exact taxonomy of devotion is—

csontképződés / ossification.

How our bones (rusted peafowl-blue) train-rattle arthritic like branches
familiar with exquisite abscission. What's left of you NAGYMAMA
if not a bosom of sugar with which to dust the crescent-shaped
sweet-bread of inherited grief-porcelain? What's left of
NAGYPAPA's lánytestvérek if not inflammation,

darázsfészek / a nest of wasps,

neuropathic extremity after neuropathic extremity? My skin is wreath-making.
I suffer vulturous globe thistles. Amethyst-skulled. Hook-leafed.
I suffer a thousand celestial arrows, lost in that labyrinthine
meanwhile you spell-casted. And you are no longer here
peace-offering pain: eperdzsem cédrusfa százszorszép pitypang.

Mackenzie Schubert Polonyi Donnelly

Dear Aceso

*

Now I whistle the body's spectral wasps home
for telluric vespers. A swarm twinkling with little cowbells.
A constellation coruscating
birdsong-silver like windchimes.
Anatomy is weather-vaned
earthward. The ancestral velvet of
apricots, my very own skin. Vascular cobwebs—
no enchanted corn-broom can loosen this latticed silk.
My hands, such tricolor violets of seabeds.
My hands, thick wildernesses of fringed orchids.
A peripheral pain of pinwheels, of windmills, exquisite.
I am struck arrow after arrow until
my interior becomes honeycombed like a pomegranate.
I am seasick. As if the delicate iridescence of opals.
My collagenic scaffolding suddenly sea-dwelling.
O spired crystalline cathedral.
If I remember music at all
then it must be the thistle-blue acoustics
of plumaged whales,
then it must be the body's ancient eaves
irised with survival so salival, so ligneous, so brumal.
A survival so feminine; sheathed in wings.

*

A survival so feminine; sheathed in wings.
Irised with survival so salival, so ligneous, so brumal.
Then it must be the body's ancient eaves
of plumaged whales,
then it must be the thistle-blue acoustics,
if I remember music at all,
O spired crystalline cathedral.
My collagenic scaffolding suddenly sea-dwelling;
I am seasick. As if the delicate iridescence of opals,
my interior becomes honeycombed. Like a pomegranate,
I am struck. Arrow after arrow until
a peripheral pain of pinwheels, of windmills. Exquisite,
my hands, thick wildernesses of fringed orchids,
my hands, such tricolor violets of seabeds.
No enchanted corn-broom can loosen this. Latticed silk,
apricots, my very own. Skin, vascular cobwebs—
earthward. The ancestral velvet of
anatomy is weather-vaned;
birdsong-silver like windchimes.
A constellation coruscating
for telluric vespers. A swarm twinkling with little cowbells.
Now I whistle. The body's spectral wasps, home.

Kérés krémes

15 dkg cukor, 1 egész
olvasztott méz, 4
vaj vagy zsír,
korbona.
Egy edénybe

sheathed in

ancient

music

felmelegítjük
kihűlt 45 dkg

I am

30 percig áll
sütünk ki

Töltelék

my very own

ancestral

5 dl tejben 5 evőka
rünk 20 dkg vajal
habosra keverünk és a
hozzákeverjük. 1 csomag
1 citrom reszelt héjával

Exquisite

home

26

Maija Rhee Devine

Autumn

It's a coloring contest. Red, yellow, cabernet sauvignon.
Eighty-feet-tall Zelkova Trees chew bits off the autumn sky.
Addicted to the hot sauce in the sunlight,
all day, they imbibe, get wasted.
At night, they drink stars, a cooling libation.

s. d. lishan

October 23

A bird be-
smirched chigger
in the jaw-
chucked morning.

The teeth of repeat,
a trimmed pinch,
a chink of plinth
upon which morning

builds, winched taut,
like an echoing rat-
chet. A rough-cheeked
Choctaw wince, unwept,

silence stubbed, stubbled
as milkweed stalks slit through
a grey church-stone sky.
A rattle etched, edged

flint of heap,
whipped and bewitched
amongst the unchipped,
gaggle of scratch.

Christopher Buckley

Agnostic

> I tell her I'm an agnostic
> and couldn't sleep . . .
> —Luis Omar Salinas

And what
      if looking out the window at nothing,
            at a blank horizon,
I see I've been saying the same thing
         all along . . .
            re-casting
that flicker of light
      that once burned in my chest
            like one of those
martyrs on Holy Cards
      handed out in grade school,
the ones that had them ascending
        on clouds
          into a lustrous sky
I can still see above
      our first house on Humphrey Road?
I'd always had my doubts
      about everything
         unloaded on us
weekdays to Sunday
      from the mildewed storeroom
         of sanctity.
And whatever
      was glowing in me then
        was not wisdom,

nor a cloud silver with grace,
                        not the first thing close
to free thinking . . .
                    but running across the fields
                                            I had some idea
what my glowing
                blood was worth,
                            and filled my arms full
of alyssum, wild nasturtiums,
                            and the violet glory of dusk,
out past the dark
                shoulders of the oaks,
                                    useless even to myself,
stubborn as the stars
                    always slow to appear. . . .
                                        One way or
the other,
        I'm still here,
                halfway sure of nothing,
                                and don't think
there's anywhere else
                I could be,
                        which more or less takes care of
metaphysics and all
                its replacement parts. . . .

                                *

You can send your heart off
                        with the supplication of the clouds

and see where that gets you—

                        probably not past the black and white

films of the lives of saints

                  showed repeatedly

                            on rainy days

all through the '50s. . . .

                Now I let my thoughts roll

                            past leaves

of the liquidambars

                already red as flames

                        in September, even here,

or especially here, in California. . . .

                    I wonder what spheres

Giordano Bruno saw

              as he first breathed in

                      the smoke rising

beneath his feet

            in the Campo de' Fiori—

                      did the Inquisitors think

they'd done away with uncertainty,

                the plurality of worlds?

Aren't we all riding the hard rails

              of light out of here

                    and not

coming back,

        given the quantum heresies

                in wind?

And no matter how much we sing

            about a starry crown,

isn't the last tune we hear one of dust—

                                not a wisp of evidence

that prayers have risen

               beyond the ionosphere?

                *

I give a little more away

             to that wind each day,

                         and to the birds

who arrive on its coattails, scroungers

                       like the rest of us.

If I fished,

        I could fish all day,

                 but I'd rather walk along the shore

where there's nothing new

             beneath the sky,

                  where I have no memory

of another life

          in which the stars were useful. . . .

If I was promised something

             it has never found me here,

on this bench above the sea,

             though such absence

                  doesn't mock me

any more than the distance beyond the waves,

               even though

I'm still a serious man

       half the time,

            for no good reason

I can think of. . . .

As far as I can see,

we're on our own,

like the coral trees

or the Spanish palms

tangled in fog. . . .

Cynthia Bargar

Atonement after Sunset at Ponyhenge

There is no thou to speak of.
          —Lucie Brock-Broido

No burial for these beloved remains. No breath, no whinny,
No neigh. No dusty attic. No cellar, damp. No landfill.
No capture. No pasture grasses bolster molded stallions.
No saddle soap, no stable roses. No frills festoon the wooden
Ones on rocker rails, with tufts of straw for tails. No midway,
No corral, no pony pokey. No rough beasts slouching
Save for hobby horses & rocking ponies. No
Theologies but their rounding-the-bend mythologies.

                              In their heyday I was young
& they were all the rage, yet I never wanted one.   Today, I
Pilgrim to the field where they circle. Praise their saviors,
Seek to redeem myself.   The sun sets.
It's the eve of tomorrow   sacred day.

                    Are there not at least 100 ways to pray.

Arthur Solway

Mid-Autumn Diary

September

There was a birdcage
without its bird
and the unlatched window.
I closed my eyes.

October

The rocking horse
was going nowhere.
And a sliver of mid-autumn moonlight
crept across the floor.

November

Only the shadows creaked—
nothing else.
Not even those black gloves
of night could hold us.

Gillian Cummings

As Sleep Comes

The sound of a thousand starlings
from a canopy of maple, winged.

If it comes as sleep comes,
like seeds before winter.

The thread of wind unclosing knots
of tinged orange, as maple thins.

If it comes to me like last hope,
like a canoe over dusked lake.

And inside a child rowing
to the sound of starlings, rising.

Becka Mara McKay

The Judgment of the Open Pit (*Exodus 21:23*)

All trees belong to a network, but grasses
are a mass of something else, an exodus

left in place. When the angel shuts his mouth
the weirdest things happen. He window shops,

he tears his robes in his sleep. He wipes his hands
on wool and waits to hear the shofar blow.

When did you first notice these symptoms? When
I saw the bright book and winter jumped in front.

What did our ancestors do when the Levites
got gout, when the body's burdens shouldered

God past diaspora? Coyotes are both
temporary blemish and permanent

trouble, like the bird of your voice at night.
The sound engineer put his hand up my

sweater to better engineer the sound
of my voice without implicating my skin.

William Orem

The Festal Letters

The silence at the last leaf
of Mark's evangel,
when no one knows, or tells, what has befallen;

the way *Letter to the Romans* says nothing
of a man from hill country

                   but only announces his absence, here.

The fact that galaxies
contain their gaps,

      sometimes, ten trillion miles of void:

         and the stars are not letters

         and the letters of the saints
     contain
            caesura.

This is why

this morning's light pressed its hands against the gate
saffron as a monk's garment,

light that is nothing but through which all colored things
arrive. This is why

the raked sky has announced a gentle rain
all early afternoon off Cape Cod,

and last night just at evensong the lichen-colored
spines of whales
pushed like lovers through grey mist.

William Barnes

the art of collage

choose your color. fold the page. fold again.
now. tear from the corners.

if you lie level with the water at dusk, at the very edge, you can see the hatch.
tiny white sails peel through the surfaces, then float, clear for a moment,—

then leap into the air.

make crescents and circles and squares.
make triangles. save the pieces.

sometimes you come to a place where the pinecones have fallen together
into a shallow bowl. fitted perfectly to the curve of the ground. as if they had been calling

each-to-each. one-and-one-and-one.

make a pile of the shapes and colors. let them drift. let them settle.
the days may pass. then weeks.

you might decide to stay. by the creekbank. to name the shallows, the greens.
sometimes you find a strangeness there. sometimes it comes in torrents.

and when you return. after the rain. look for the shapes that fit. the colors that glow. side-by-side.
look at the edges.

once, I caught a fish, far and high away. the country was granite
and pine. the waters made amber by the gravel inside.

look where the fibers come loose. sometimes clustered together. sometimes crosswise, overlapping.
the tear is ragged, uneven. look how the texture of the page rises from within.

brook trout. gravid. barely the length of my hand. a flashing white streak
at the edge of the fin. and then a thin black line. and then crimson.

there's a landscape inside. contour. look: you can see where the cut softens
at the edge. where the paper comes undone. it beckons. into the space between

as if to reach across. leaning. toward and through.

and something else. —something muscular and strong. fluid
and wild. —her body pours into the hollows.

take these. and the stream-colored light. —the pathway's circling.
—and falling the way it does through the trees.

Brenda Beardsley

troglodyte

beg to disappear, enter your cave. there are margins, where grey rocks skim
metamorphic remains, your entirety, diminishing

this; how soul leaks into soil: pour enough want into a pot & what empties—
the amniotic, a friction of leaves: wet, willowy, wondering, stained

for your margins are this now before the cleft & palate of what spikes
retreat, wounds the embryotic, calcifies, & you leak

what tears contain; this lake is unheart, where leaves fluster
cilia sweeping, redirecting; diminishing

for this, a womb which entrusts soul; dolomite protectant—
what pains, now cease.

Notes:
https://wasg.org.au/index.php/2015-09-05-08-07-15/2016-06-27-13-46-34/glossary-of-caving-terms

after Susan Stewart, "The Forest"

Kristina Erny

Shuttle

Who threw all that robust confetti into the trees
overnight? Burnt toffee, magenta, bloodroot.
What thrums at the edge of a pasture, a thin
country stretch called Short Shun, a one-lane
bridge?

The margin, like, above the rush of the road
could an astronaut tilting her face sideways to
get a better eyeball on the earth see each leaf
cluster, see us coming now through the mist
pocket, how the morning's foam has gone cold?

Pull up a chair, Mama, this picture's for you,
my daughter says, when she hands me the
moon, cratered with grey pepperoni and her
name perfect, all caps and underlined. *P - H -
Y - L - L - I - N - A* tilted around the
circumference of her picture like a question.

Who is swiftly disappearing? Whose twin is
balanced now in the sky like a thimble on an
ochre plate? *Morning, God*! I can see us
spinning there over the field, steady as
chameleons, the leaves like orange eyes
looking: look at us, how we are.

The corn stalks have already been broken.
And we are still sunburnt from summer, and
gathered together, passing by changing trees.

Michael Chitwood

Falling Leaves Catching in Fallen Leaves

Ah, the confetti of it all.
The scrolling on air. County Fair time
and more than a little Frostian
if your teeth will take it.
It's like they do this every year
and every year we fall for it,
Autumn musking in from the pumpkin truck.
The rake's got tines on it's hand
and a waltz if you've got it in you.
The poplar and dogwood shimmy,
a breeze striptease.
Lawdy mama gimme some gaudy.
No two roads here. Just the one.

Deborah Gorlin

Aging in Place

Cows down the road, steady Eddies, sunken in mud,
plodding, unfazed whatever the weather is
or his diagnosis, her blood disorder. Still milking.
The sun, even when hidden. Those goats nosing
the fence, curious, in greeting, whenever I visit.
Stones in partial walls mossed over, softening lichen.
And while the rusting harrow is useless, set on the grass
for display, it is an instructive fossil. Blued wild apples
glow in the darkness, dimly electric. Pigs rest
in their stys, enjoy them, and the horses stanchioned,
at least for now, are curried quiet. Worry can be
made into warm sweaters. At least that, darling!
From my kitchen window, the barn's red walls tilt
like cards and like my heart will break. And perhaps
what's after, the clean sweep of the fields, maybe cover
of rye to stay the soil from flight, under the wide-open
no-contest sky, and a horizon, hard to make out but hoped
for, heaven already. Me, nowhere in sight, inside
gorgeous autumn, when the bright leaves clap
wildly, uproariously, falling down laughing.

Annette Sisson

At sixteen, instead of practicing piano

I drifted through back acres
      to the tree line, wove
          through dry brush around
a downed sugar maple,
      soft bark spread
          across clover and nutsedge, sinking
to humus. Fiery leaves
      scattered like light, tongued
          the bright air. A fallen
pin oak draped the bounding
      creek. I swayed and balanced
          along its trunk, alighted
in denser shade, untied
      sweatshirt from waist, head
          and arms into fleece—then straddled
a crumbling elm, grooves
      and knots poking through heavy
          denim. Sparrow, jay,
cardinal, squirrel, constant
      as the stream wending over
          under twig and stone,
thoughtlessly making its way.
      I opened my journal, bent
          to the page, became acorn,
goldenrod, crow—waves
      of words skimmed paper
          and breeze. I lifted my eyes—
low sun straight
      ahead, a dark slash
          of limb stenciled silver.

Cows wailed in pastures
      beyond the trees—I heard
         my mother call to me,
one of her last petitions,
      as if she might launch
         into song, dark lament,
flume of water churning.

Karen Earle

[dew-starred]

dew-starred
web-and-window

autumn: what was
returns   in owl-light

rain-caressed
tree trunks   rise

dark   through
leaf-loud   drumming

scrape-waltz   a bit
wind-thistled

this browning
we gather   woolens

darkest weave   spider
story   beehive

history   all
honey and sting

Laura Budofsky Wisniewski

Math Sonnet #1

translated from Dreamath

I am Patient 31. From my spot,
this single cot, I see the squares inside squares
of the Sanitarium. Illness divides my body
from my body, as the late October shadows

divide daylight from the day. Let
the call of a few wild geese, still free,
equal the cry of an unknown constant;
otherwise, what we have lost will be greater

than the sum of what remains. What remains?
The imaginary numbers of summer;
the future's null set of desires, shapeless
as these half-empty pajamas; and

the anger, a winged and fervent creature,
solving, solving for a new X to live for.

Math (Snt) #1

#31/illness = daylight/day
C(cry of wild geese) = Y
i#summer + o[(future(desire)] + A(anger) < Sum (loss)
A(anger) [?] = X {to live for}

Laura Budofsky Wisniewski

When the Leaves Have Fallen, the Zen Master Stops Eating

Dawn lies down with him,
his wrist cupped in Nurse Lynn's hand.
He has departed

his thin bones, broken
into a hundred small clouds.
A light rain begins,

quenching the dead leaves,
filling the shallow puddles,
drenching the milkweed. Yet

still we sit waiting
we, his empty bowls.

Marjorie Maddox

Midlife Mowing

No mercy for the fallen:
mulched and spit out on flat grass
now littered with what once were leaves
arrogant in their acrobatic twirls
from twig to dirt.
    What did they know
of us, who once loved them,
rollicking in the *Ah!* of autumn,
their colorful pyramids piled so high
we thought—by diving courageously
into what we couldn't see beneath—
we hid who we really were:
frightened, naïve?
    What did we know
of who we would become,
    here in the backyard
of middle age, navigating the ten-year
mower around a fenced-in square
of nostalgia that we've meticulously
cut and trimmed into a fashion
    of the childhood
we've somehow forgotten we left
locked in the old shed behind
the cracked croquet set,
the tattered badminton net,
the busted sled, the rusting rake,
    the latter replaced
by the heave-ho of our breath
as we round the last stretch
of leaves now huddled and waiting

for the nonchalant execution
we promised we'd never deliver?

Jenny Grassl

Earth Sings Greensleeves to Mankind

Alas my love you do me wrong / To cast me off so discourteously / And I have loved you so long / Delighting in your company . . . / I have been ready at your hand / To grant whatever thou wouldst crave. I have waged both life and land / Your love and goodwill for to have

    1. touchstone   mark heart with rock to be sure of karat

    2. score light to be certain of darkness

    3. touch wood   fearing animal   vegetable outcomes

    4. collect evidence—one leaf— cells row sugar

    from stem to tip   many leaves canceling summer

my trees drop messages to your children   jumping in

raked heaps   brittle music of repeat   repeat   deaf

but for what they hear   battle of love letters

long-distance kiss   breaking up   with the throats

of geese   and worry interval of train whistle

they do understand   my season   but not how

things fall   let me just say to them— love is high

then deep   piles you land in   hitting dirt

your weight in the weightless   and still you mourn

only hyacinths   the bulbs sleepwalking below

how shall I cover myself in pink and blue   after leaving

Susan McCabe

Ovid Speaks to Bark, in These Times of Our Sickness

That Sycamore might be a woman who dropped her leaves,
crispy bark without thinking leaves are rashes   yellow spotted mud-red-veined each
thousands of pores, mouths. I can
breathe change into
        gods   vegetables insects   animals that perfoliate
in every air or mood—Dancing,
white blood cells rush everywhere on call. Cordyceps with caterpillar
fingers I am.   I asked to be a reed, a lily, an eel. I wanted to be that forever
autumn, then that spider dreaming without eyesight biting
flesh for germination.   A virus travels restlessly . . .
Chemistry inhabits and inhibits.
        I am the bride of wholeness while everywhere bits and pieces swim.
For it takes one to live one—to taste disintegration
when the sylvan one kisses me
under cliff heights, I am the groom to
lymph lakes guarded by nymphs, yet they too
        grow weary, numbers not in on the almost
        dead. Send the mermaids to the basement to practice on
xylophones, let them spike their hair with magenta. Time to let go
 of cellular waste. I learned to read in the haste of margins:
        letters swivel ants so tasty to nibble, another cloud
out of a sky's sentence:
Cloud, cloud, cloud—gaps between—Cirrus crisis,
then the Altostratus.
                    Air erases what it can.
That woman, of course, is a Sycamore who dropped her leaves.
The bark tastes sweet like darkness—be
the woman choosing to be lost in unkempt woods—
finding herself in rain, alcohol, the last rivulet—
Awareness takes all that flows. It must. Hurt color too.

The mannequin I thought to become walked off the day a
statue of Artemis arrived, direct, flat, bony
with arrow pointing away from Urgent Care. The care
of the man who wears a pizza box as a sun hat,
dragging entrails of garbage can to can't.
This hatches something
else. Something can grow a branch, or hoof, or
act like it does, like
not taking a drug for a drug-like effect. This injection can evolve.
All can dissolve
into variants mutating, wanting Apollo's cure:
the prickly pear or the cashmere clouds. His solar blazed
several epidemics . . .
. . .
Infirmaries are nurseries, seedlings born
too soon, must
survive frigidity, coughing redness.
                              I see a dark canal and then I am one.
I see my photo of a tree-tall Sunflower but Siri says she can't use past days.
A mesh holds across wind-withering gullies. More leaves. Can you
write to me what to become next . . .

Katherine Cota MacDonald

Sundust

Peach *a pêche.*
It begins with fresh
ripe running waters from the flesh,
cloud-edges warmed and warming,
léchez,
s'il vous plaît, avec ce soleil—

Mais maintenant? Il fait froid.
Each day, ill-fated fraud,
the sun, as it winds down dancing,
sweaty sway as skin cools and the gossamer
striking out of the parcels and pods softens the blow
of the collecting distance,
asclépiade,
des pieds—
the rustling quiets.

Peach season is done,
the pits shorn bare
while milkweed grows its moonlit hair.
The sundust settles,
le laiteron,
oh, but later on,
les dents du lion—

I sink my teeth, my whole self, into this housepod,
with winter's fracture-painted windows,
left with a frost tucked into a husk,
hollow and hauling,
for peach season once again:

My tusks tearing into greenery,
Dandelion, Tussock, Tiger,
this bonechill is warmed by dreams
of wild flutters, of painted papillon.

Sarah Maclay

Swansong ~ Autumn Aubade

Valentine, Valentino, valiant, salient liqueur on that Ojai hotel table—

jodhpuring or purring, softly, just down low. Even I will wilt, while

how many times, door ajar, did you enter?

There was that moment—jet velvet and leather, turned,

entirely without azure, it seems—but skyjoining, horizon vast,

cemented; no indigo, but jade, black, tree-full, *vert*. Appropriately urned. Tell me

again of a cabin, wooded windows. Bring my morning joe—maybe Caffe Verona?

Or when you sat on my bed in that ivory cutaway—ivory and white—

just hushed-in like the 19th century, visiting and suave,

joyous, also wildly open, calm—voicing the secret purpose of conflict and

how to do it well. Just like a Baudelaire Buddha, a Valery

flaneur. An ormolu Mallarme making me achy and

free. How quietly, then, the cotton or linen must slip from one of us

onto the walking body of a child, alone, tan—the cloth now a simple shift—

golden-tressed, a girl, but with something like your eyes—co-mingled?

Or maybe unrelated. It's uncanny warm, and still. Barren sidewalk. Morning.

No one else around. No sound. She, both directed and astray. Carefully—

but how does one begin to help, to try? This pixie cut, in silence. The ficus and flame tree.

Feathers, grounded. Broken wing. In the darkening sunlight of midday.

Maybe it was then I reached for the iron fencepost, just to stand. Or maybe that was

you. Where is our windowed hotel view of city lights, from the sheets? Which city?

Our night field, those wet stars? Send back that cabin swan-around-waist-from-behind.

Luisa A. Igloria

The Myth of Distance

No creature's exempt from thirst and desire.

    So, when a friend writes *The body is
a constellation of joy*, I release

a long breath, several breaths. I too want

    to be a shape reclining on the inky canopy,
a string of garden lights tethering my left

heel to my rib bone, my scapula, my shoulder

    dome; and the line from there leading down
the wrist and to the hand, which is holding

either a pencil or a mug filled with coffee

    and froth, or a trowel and a bit of cake
on a dessert spoon. All around me, silky tufts

    of milkweed are falling at their own soft
speed. And I am not alone, I am unafraid.

John James

The Field Which Had Been a Meadow Once

Gently the cherry
blossoms shake they shake. The limbs
bend this way &
the flowers do not return.
They revolute
in ion air. *It lifts it*
lifts. The dirt is callous now.
Desiccated so
that when I look
out over the plain
what registers is a palimpsest
of dried foliage, phantomic
stumps of withered oaks
emerging like
sheared corn from the furrows
& the flat, uneven ash
where grapevines used to be.
Often I am permitted.
The oak trees lose their form.
Often I am permitted
to project this image.
Barn swallows swirl. They
lift they—Life
expands, absorbs. It tends
in directions
almost infinite. (In sunk
gutters of abandoned houses,
in breaks between concrete squares.)
Often I return to
this field which had been

a meadow once, which
like a mine in the mind
razes the eternal pasture
I still call home. My body
ages now. The grass
blows east toward the source
of the sun. *In ion air it lifts. It is*
no dream. Still the saplings
usher from the uneven earth.
Still the worm turns.
The wind still moves in concert
with the few shaking leaves, which still
photosynthesize in this
unmoving afternoon.

Alicia Rebecca Myers

Loss

I prefer the desiccated pod to the moony flower. You can make a starfish
out of five halves glued together at the base or a holiday garland
strung with sweetgum balls that save. What's more compelling than an empty shell?
The winter after my dad died, he tapered to a point, I power-walked
past a house whose overhanging second-story Christmas lights were arranged
like strings on a missing harp. The most alive I feel is when I corner death. To hold
in my hands what isn't, like the time our son brought home a drawing labeled,
Self-Portrait of What I'm Not. My dad coughed up phlegm
into a hospital napkin stained with grease. I'd smuggled bacon to give him
a final taste of fat. He couldn't swallow, just held it in his mouth, smiling. I knew
in that moment of floating goose down, third time in a month our rescue dog
turned and tore into my body, that we had to give her up. To love
anything wholly is to accept its painful winding loss. But you can make a cradle
out of a milkweed pod, use the floss as swaddling for an acorn baby.

Rosemary Herbert

In Elsie's Garden

In memory of Elsie Tiger Fruson

Buffeted,
tufted with milkweed silk
snagged in blowsy bouffant heads,
papery hydrangeas
bow to the big chill,
stiffly whispering of cereus—
strange bedfellow—
and the ecstatic one-night stand
that utterly eclipsed
month after month
of rhapsody in blue.

Libby Maxey

The New Actaeon

Deer season stains the baited woods and makes
a trap of our familiar paths. The red
and orange, predatory or a plea
against the fate of prey, are sparks of fake
and jarring autumn. We take part. Instead
of watching warm September pull and ease
the maples' yellow through the canopy,
we look for hunters' perches warily,
imagining ourselves in sights. Twilight
and we have used up all the water where
a goddess might have bathed—no wonder, then,
our hounds now turn to us for blood. Our blight
is hoarding safety, sure our rightful share
is stasis—going out as we came in.

L. Stuart

Autumn Understory

Suppose the fallen oak
sluicing through the understory

is you.
Beside a mantle of moss

Night tightens. The mechanism
of your jaw opens upon scarlet flowers.

You wear your crown of thorns
amid violets under cold elms.

An oak sapling is your staff.
You lift it toward the blue jays,

the canopy of red and gold,
the junco's twill, a war shield made of hide

left beside the milkweed, and the three deer
bringing gifts to you from the meadow at twilight.

Jon Davis

Wallace Stevens in the Blackfoot River Valley

One would want snow even as the autumnal turns
Saturnalian. One would want the knuckled limbs
made stark by sunrise. When morning's heat
leavens the wasps, they'll scrawl nonce forms
across the window's bright page while the poet cramps
over a sheaf between woodpile and flame.
In this romance, he craves a language to haunt
the ephemeral. Were he to lament, the sash
would burst into flame. Were he to celebrate, the moon
would lift above the cottonwoods abetting the creek,
the lone coyote would lance through high grass,
and the grizzly would sway, golden in that dawn.
The actual carries an exhausted charm mitigated
only by the imagination's refusal. What the poet sees
is a measure of his pain. What he hopes to see, a measure
of his mortality. He bears the cross of the imagination
over the hills of the actual. When he finally writes,
there is no fire, no grizzly, no cottonwood, no coyote.

Gibson Fay-LeBlanc

From Room to Room

—for Jane Kenyon

At this ungodly hour the windows of a room reflect inside: a ceiling like a wooden floor
and not the dark street, the giant, still trees.

At this hour it seems possible for my mind to not be a wind-up monkey though that beast
woke me by banging my skull with grievances and other forgotten songs.

Late fall. Strong coffee, a fire, a book; light soon, and a poet calls with her barn,
abandoned hoe, and darkening *scoop in the oats*.

What if she'd lived? If we met now and startled ourselves by stumbling through
small talk, would we have wound our way around to the fact that we were born
on the same date, both met our beloveds young, left the Midwest for their New
England, spent years among other people's people?

Cancer took her and took the poems she would have written, as it took whatever
else it was my brother might have written, locked in that same room of illness
where each thing—notebook, pen, lamp—is sharp and seen for what it is.

This disease that turns a body's will to create against itself.

If she had walked out of that room, wrote more, she would be seventy-two and exiting a
tunnel of grief for her lost love, lion, rural engine, now gone two years.

We do not recover such losses; we learn to sit with them in a room.

I'm writing her a note with my own list of these plainly lit particulars, now visible in the
dawn I've watched rise again—a small comfort for comfort she's given me:

a strip of silver maple,
a baseball with a country of leather peeled off,
a wooden-handled edger against the garage wall.

Veronica Patterson

Autumn Is a Honey Locust Tree

—for Evan

If autumn is a honey locust tree, and it is,
then winter is each bared-branch threshold of the sky.
The tree shades us in summer. Grief is

the lake behind the house. & contentment is a sentinel—
the great blue heron that gathers gulls and egrets
to pooled fish. But not us. The once-born child, a gamin

who loved the world, as she did—its blue wild geranium
blossoms, is still named Megan. Her brief dark hair
sprouted fragile hope. & her hours become a book

crusted with salt. I spend years walking every
morning and returning to you. To her. We canoe
on the happy gleam of lake, paddling, as we do,

gently. We litany the names of mountains to the west.
Sometimes we, and we do, hold each other & feel
three hearts beat. When lakeshore appears in fall

we descend the rip-rap to skip flat rocks two or three
or seven times, each a sinking dream. We are
learning to watch the ripples, which never exactly end.

Calleja Smiley Welsh

The tree and I have nothing

against each other. At my back, its bark
is rough, a background impression no less thick

and jagged for residing at the edges
or among the drift of leaves in the sun-

streaked morning. Is it naïve—can it be ok
to enjoy the mulchy waft

of final days, this line of burnished trees,
the clear bird call—suppose

only this leaf? Each one tenders me
an absent lover. How long should I wear black

while the funeral remains
endless, the mourning period no longer

defined. What to honor the dead when the flowers
too are fading. Who, the dead—

me, my children, my children's children,
this maple sapling, this cricket, the sometime

regal fritillary and bluebreast darter?
I am liable to touch them

without reason, and with just a touch
of desperation. An ineffectual gesture,

finally, to drop my hands
to the ground, fling my listening

to the bird-loud canopy. To rely on a tree
and insist in dirt only lashes myself to the coming

conflagration, our crowns the shedding red
of overbloom.

Mara Adamitz Scrupe

Lawrence Campground Windfall Orchard

moreover   Jack Pines would have no
place here—in their windbreak/ in their soughing & sighing
          resistance—with the orchard in its half-dozen

perfect rows   would have no reason to cry
out in unison with these fruit trees in their seventy-five years'
sustenance   *take & eat of us*   *for we are your very flesh*

your quiddity   & likewise as we position our bodies
          conditioning what we intuit internally/ once wet-
painted/ anciently embedded in lime & marble dust/ lambent as Minoan
          alabaster or bright sparkling as the Kansas Little Jerusalem

badlands—untouched/ bleak &

hindering—unlike the lost tallgrass prairie   more than
one hundred million acres vanished forever as the tender
          care Grandpa gave his peonies & three granddaughters

but would not   could not   extend
          to his only son   *—too timid*   *too effeminate—*

& so I live in my mourning body   and his
& in the last leavings of my grandfather's nursery/ his viewshed
          —what he saw when he looked out—   I feel most
acutely the necessity to celebrate the gifts that come & I reconsider

          as hindsight the flood that both Cuvier & Buckland
tried to date—post-biblical—from a pile of paleoanthropological
          rubble: ante or prediluvian?   & contrarily in clamant

sympathy for these apple trees' dignity & how
        they've stood alone for what must seem   to them
        like fifty thousand years of bearing

bearing—who planted them/ nurtured them/ & who in death
        deserted them?—   withal

        as the philosopher once said   *we are all lost*
creatures & I sense the night *the night* in vibrations of our earth's
thunderous turning   *turning*   & in the heritable

                —gathering windfall—   I think

        how we all change   & how *my apple*
trees endure at a KOA campground on a former farm field
        as everywhere everything else crumbles/ everything
        succumbs & I grieve the wasted wasp-bit half-mush I left

        left behind   & I keenly recall autumn's blushing
incandescence & best commend in numinous spirit
        in preservation/ perpetuation   these heirloom Winesaps

I put up   —thirteen quarts in all of the sweetest
        ever applesauce—living as though I'm on the road
forever in this tiny trailer   I now call home

Natalie Taylor

Shouldering into Rest

Beaver Moon: November 8, 2022

The leaves, the leaves, the leaves—glorious technicolor lighting long
autumn afternoons. Faint rustle of husk brushing earth. Sky clear above
flame. Snake dreams, delicate scales gliding over mud, slick foliage, around
the frozen egg, unhatched under stone.

Dim crack, stem splits from
limb before spilling into
space. A settling sigh.

First dusting of snow and its singular quiet.
Hush people, please hush.
Let the forest breathe.
Let the owl perch on her wooden sword.
Let the beaver's orange teeth whittle willow.
Let the moon bleed in earth's shadow.
Let the dark wrap around the trees until we wake again.
Let the vermillion stars chant with their pointed tongues.

Steven Salmoni

Landscape, with Changing Weather

It's difficult to see, in the wheeling sun, the sky, in all its mineral colors.
This sky is a slight November,

and who can say if the umbrellas predict the coming storm? Who can
pretend to be "the nothing that was, however, unexpected?"

After every divination, the present becomes less known, as if it were the
nature that one sees.

Is this true? Can we decorate "the flat rain-barrier, with its intimations of a
wrought-iron fence?"

I suppose it is winter because we dreamed the hope of being literal.

The body we formed was given, in return for that which said nothing, and
which had no effect upon our return. Sapling nerve, renamed in stone,

the clouds' desire, the same land over land promised in the silhouette.

I would lend myself this figure, derived from the prior season, the verge of
continuity with summer, to return in the manner of being anywhere.

But look at the clouds carried away by the horizon which adopts them.
I suppose it was the silhouette on grey, beams applied to wind in their
graphic construct.

Or, clouds come before the clouds; it's difficult to say. Firm in their hold,
although I'd make no suggestions,

as we always return to a sun that we recognize—a sun, like the sun that at
the same instant flew away.

The layers of white were horizontal,

and the splintered branches lay upon the road, beneath those skies as they all were caught between the branches. Then one became the opposite of rain, the opposite of sky. As if one's life had been reversed and permanently re-tried upon the heathered wall. As we were, withdrawn to that self-same place.

The time to draw the scene would reveal that we were already and the day seemingly declining, seemingly a lie. Are the broken man's branches not the branches of another's change? There is an empty field that is still as empty as it was when all the snow lay upon the ground.

Every stalk turns to a branch gone missing, and when the roof was covered in white, the silver branch had no "sea-breaking fire that could still the moon." The scene was thus enframed, and yet all within would reach beyond such limits, and we too were both above and below the bend in the horizon.

What, then, is fixed in space when we proceed from this fixed point between us? We have no nature in the lines that we desire, all based upon the myth that if one attempts to climb the hill, one might, at the last minute, change it. The palms of our hands would sound the depths, and limbs

gather in more elevated prospects, and we must make something more permanently blue, with the grey that is barely more than a hill, with the horizon enshadowed, even as it comes more into our possession, even when each branch would remember every other.

The shallow north fretted. "Where have you been all the time?"

"How can you ask?" I would land anywhere. This doesn't count, because I believe in mountains. It was a natural mistake, a time to recall the condition of things, to look neither right nor left, and with the sun that we recognized and that the recognition was a subject that flew away from subject. Houses, cloud-shapes, struck across the sky, white houses, and cream-colored houses, given up and landing where the world would not adopt them.

"Meanwhile, I intend everything." Clouds before September, as we last were in July, some shades lighter than the light upon. There will be islands—if not to-day, then another day. "Beauty defies what it would otherwise affect." It's the bare idea that makes you. Even as the day made no suggestions of its own.

Replace that sky with sky, and it's never the year that we made ourselves. No more conclusions than what the landscapes in relief have authorized. I receive the title: "it is me," as I am bound.

But then, "why am I flying?" The roof slopes beyond the roof, only for itself; isn't that you?

Yes, that's it; confess to the seasons that the seasons are enough, the divination that reveals how we'll pass beyond its accident. "One just becomes, etc." ourselves "unfolding as if within ourselves," and one's reply, a thousand pages long, and what devices came, through which the plane that threw me feinted, as the prism concentrates each being to its array of exemplary, streaming lights.

Have mercy; not every door should mourn the misted limbs where a celestial eyelid hovers on the border. It's what makes us curious, without having to imagine that we should drag ourselves each Sunday, that we might have some relief, that the gestures you make are mine, or that I should have something to sign, to find a thread, "to cast" you said "upon a silent spar."

Rebecca A. Durham

Wood Parade

Pour, pour down matter   like lava flowing into rock

pour through   like air whisked through slot canyons

     carved sandstone snaking   below rivers of sky

   striated   like waves on silt

       cobalt light lashes over wood grains

layers notch time with lignin

         each year rung like a badge

light   expanse following   a dark stop

         now atoms rearrange

            bonds heat-singed

    pyrolysis

         atoms and energy   release

unbound atoms now hot blue   mingle with ambient O_2

   glowing gas   not the former tree   spooky blue

     vibrations become heat

   a fire whorl

                              orange
              dervish

              flickering   with life-pulse

cindered

        &   smoke licked

                  these breakages

years   unraveling into ash

            &

            a red rift

Lisa Furmanski

primer of prairie portent

Basket of fountain thistle. From fritillary
and wallflower, a basket. Dwarf-flax, thorn mint, bluestem,
a basket. For sake of tasks, a basket,

for sake of weaving that latticed. Every strand
plucked and spoked. The tightest clasped sand
to wrap the stoves. For sake of

blue grama, buffalo, soapweed—flicking
the bison sequined with flies. Forsaken, the native

grasses—for sake of maize. No whispered grooves

for snakes, no roots netting water so dust stays land.
Drought for the long middle, mute in the rain—

                            desolation,

swallowing the fist of itself. For sake of susurrus!
Cornstalks sigh, not grass,
                not wild, in glossed, soldiering rows.

Preeti Parikh

The [   ] of Form

Form is—

caress

two backyard kathal trees
jamun at the front boundary wall
gulmohar fronds strewn across the verandah
aam and neem canopying the courtyard

flow

wet   paint smell
faint veins   of color stains
a tremoring hand   beads   of sweat
grandfather's   old chair

hiatus
a receptacle   of absence

lines   blankness   margins

Gray's Textbook of Anatomy
a partially digested meal   of thoughts   ruminating

an eye
a mouth that hisses: You observe much   too much

muck

damp soccer field
bale of turtles   sunning on a slimy log
opacity and translucence   on an X-Ray film

urge   *mouthfeel*

instrument of the mind
syllables   new language in an oral cavity
umami of acceptance on tongue

fecund

feral dogs   vultures   urban landfill
brown-black pollutant-leached groundwater
a jhola spun   from washed and upcycled plastic strips

unguent

tall elephant grass   heated tar roads
peafowl   lit embers in a coal stove
the Brahmaputra   afar
spilling   into its flooding basin

fragment

snatched artifact   a wound
keloiding   itself   into repair

mould

lyric   language   stanzaic
retained   armored
partitioned   [b r e a c h]able

                                                  integument

                 an anatomy   of silence   the answer
                                  to "what if"

                                          selvage
                      unraveling   as if

gash

Ordovician gorge   river   of melting glaciers
heron   folding wings midair

[   ]*'s averted gaze*
engrossed   unreachable

                              testimony

                                   betrayal

                 a holy river
                            its burning banks
           I'd like to cremate   a corpse there
              the corpse
                            of my diffidence

Rick Hilles

Prayer for This Morning

All's regeneration, everything
                                     alive
on this first day
                  of December

the leaf & foot patterns

in grassy mud start to freeze

But the light's still finding us

high in the sky
                  over everything

& I still see
          the colors of last season

Autumn reds   lime-yellow greens

all around for us to see

And the cold air remains   still

as if contemplating   mercy
were its work today
               & not every day

The thigh-thick trees
                hold up the sky

And the river to my left
                carries light

And I realize
        that I'm walking with it all

back into my life, coming with me

even as it shimmers
                into darkness

G. C. Waldrep

Autumn Celebrant

*

shafts of music
in condescension

a common
syntax, acts
shepherd boldly

lament—
reclaim—compel

*

mered
into city, into
the apex-plank—

*

in plenitude, or
whereas
(& yet among)
           hence

answer

(kind Scioto,
yr bronzed gate)

*

chafed wing
in darkness,
a new concession

its indulgences
summoning
winter's prophecy

*

vacuum-drone
or pitch
below which
everything falls

small wheat
to the inner ear

*

unmarrow me,
herdling

(the pietist trees
uprooted, as
from a storm)

*

permutation
upon permutation

(amidst
the dried grasses)

*

the garden
returns to you
(it seems)
as song-in-stone

the root
& its entourage

*

the dewpoint's
rhythm

in deep-
set expectation—

*

G. C. Waldrep

Resting Crown

Emplumed milkweed seed at rest
on the eyelid of a deer.

The deer is dead. The seed, waiting
inside its anticipatory
joy.

*Around the body / hairs sharpen
light*, Leila Wilson wrote.

I bring my warmth to its warmth
as to its non-warmth,
which hovers inside the moment.

Squander, a new word for nothing
I know.

What I know falls, rises, & falls
again, the open eye a tent it passes

en route to the fire
breaking the compact observatory
I place my hand beneath.

I am a rich man, by some measures.

The joy
as it, the seed, luffs again,
non-intersecting, impartible, a toll.

G. C. Waldrep

Milkweed Remnant, Colton Point Road

the dream of winter,
tucked inside
the womb of self

it is reversible
(like all knowledge)

it chants my name
at the slowest tempo
it makes of me
a monosyllable

the milkweed's
expired zodiac,
ascendant, recollects
the blind fissure

adhering
to the accidental

sharp or flat making
way for the
tongue's brute axis

faith's torsion
amidst the material
acquires a certain
matte finish
the self speaks into

oh no cry the ghosts
not another
poem about blame

CONTRIBUTORS

rose auslander

rose auslander lives on Cape Cod and is addicted to water and poetry (not necessarily in that order). Her book *Wild Water Child* won the 2016 Bass River Press Poetry Contest; her chapbooks include *Folding Water*, *Hints*, and *The Dolphin in the Gowanus*; and look for her poems in *Berkeley Poetry Review*, *Chicago Quarterly Review*, *Atlanta Review*, *Baltimore Review*, *New Ohio Review*, *New American Writing*, *LEON*, *Rhino*, *Roanoke Review*, *Tinderbox*, and *Tupelo Quarterly*, among others. She earned her MFA in Poetry at Warren Wilson.

Cynthia Bargar

Cynthia Bargar is the author of *Sleeping in the Dead Girl's Room* (Lily Poetry Review Books), selected as a Massachusetts Book Awards 2023 Honors Poetry Book. Her poems have appeared or are forthcoming in many journals including *Ocean State Review*, *SWWIM Every Day*, *Driftwood Press*, *On the Seawall*, *Rogue Agent*, *Book of Matches*, *Sugar House Review*, and in *Our Provincetown: Intimate Portraits*, a book of images and text by Barbara E. Cohen (Provincetown Arts Press, 2021). Cynthia is associate poetry editor at *Pangyrus*. "Atonement After Sunset at Ponyhenge" was first published in the *Lily Poetry Review*. www.cynthiabargar.com.

William Barnes

Will Barnes is deputy director of the Surface Resources Division at the New Mexico State Land Office in Santa Fe and the national winner of the 2022 Hillary Gravendyk Prize for Poetry from Inlandia Institute Press for *the artemisia*. He is also the author of *The Ledgerbook* (3: A Taos Press 2016). Recent work has appeared in *Comstock*, *Crab Creek*, *Mudfish*, *Oberon*, *Ocotillo Reviews*, and *Taos Journal of Poetry*, among others. Will holds an MFA from New York University. http://williamsbarnes.com.

Brenda Beardsley

Brenda Beardsley's work appears or is forthcoming in *Two Hawks Quarterly*, *Soundings East*, *Bryant Literary Review*, *Swamp Ape Review*, *Seneca Review*, *Paterson Literary Review*, *Permafrost*, *DASH*, *december*, *Fence*, *American Journal of Poetry*, *Examined Life Journal* (University of Iowa, Carver College of Medicine), *Pentimento*, and *wordgathering*, as well as anthologized in *COVID Spring: Granite State Pandemic Poems*. Winner of the 2020 Martha's Vineyard Institute of Creative Writing Poetry Contest, she is a two-time finalist for the Hunger Mountain Ruth Stone Poetry Prize, as well as finalist for *december*'s 2022 Jeff Marks Memorial Poetry Prize. Beardsley was selected for an Honorable Mention in the 2023 Allen Ginsberg Poetry Awards (Poetry Center at Passaic County Community College), a finalist in the 2023–2024 Poetic Justice Institute Book Prize for her hybrid manuscript "an anecdotal history of eugenics," and also received an Honorable Mention in the 2023 Seneca Review Deborah Tall Lyric Essay Book Prize for the same manuscript. Nominated for Best New Poets 2023 by *december* for her poem "Where the Redness Lives," Beardsley earned her MFA from Goddard College.

Christopher Buckley

Christopher Buckley has recently edited *Naming the Lost: The Fresno Poets—Interviews & Essays* (Stephen F. Austin State University Press, 2021). His work was selected for Best American Poetry 2021, he was a Guggenheim Fellow for 2007–2008, and he received NEA grants in poetry for 2001 and 1984. His most recent book of poetry is *One Sky to the Next*, winner of the Longleaf Press Book Prize, 2023. *Sprezzatura* is due from Lynx House Press in 2025.

Michael Chitwood

Michael Chitwood's work has received the L. E. Phillabaum Award from LSU Press, the Chaffin Award for Appalachian Writing, and the Library of Virginia Literary Award in Poetry.

Gillian Cummings

Gillian Cummings is the author of *The Owl Was a Baker's Daughter*, winner of the 2018 Colorado Prize for Poetry, and *My Dim Aviary*, winner of the 2015 Hudson Prize from Black Lawrence Press. Her most recent chapbook is *The Shy Yellow* (Dharma Pine Editions, 2023), a letterpress edition of 20 copies. Her poems have appeared in *Barrow Street*, *Cimarron Review*, *Colorado Review*, *Denver Quarterly*, *Laurel Review*, and in other journals and four anthologies, including *The Best of Tupelo Quarterly*. She lives in Catskill, New York, where she is editing her first novel and trying, tentatively, to learn to play the cello.

Jon Davis

Jon Davis is the author of fourteen books and chapbooks, including *Above the Bejeweled City* (2021) and *Fearless Now and Nameless* (2025), both from Grid Books. Davis also co-translated Iraqi poet Naseer Hassan's *Dayplaces* (Tebot Bach, 2017). He has received a Lannan Literary Award, the Lavan Prize, and two National Endowment for the Arts Fellowships. He taught creative writing for 30 years, including 28 at the Institute of American Indian Arts where he co-founded both the BFA and MFA programs. He performs with the poetry + rock band Clap the Houses Dark: clapthehousesdark.com.

Maija Rhee Devine

Maija Rhee Devine is a Korean-American poet and nonfiction and fiction writer. Her autobiographical novel about Korea, *The Voices of Heaven*, won four awards, and her TEDx Talk relaying the book's relevance to today's South Korean society's critical issues is at http://youtu.be/GFD-6JFLF5A. She received an NEA Grant, 2001. Her stories and poems have appeared in the *Kenyon Review*, *North American Review*, her chapbook *Long Walks on Short Days*, and anthologies, including *When the Virus Came Calling: COVID-19 Strikes America* (Golden Foothills Press, 2020). The Smithsonian Institution featured her story in its *Folk Life Magazine* of May 13, 2022: https://folklife.si.edu/magazine/korean-happiness-screen-daughter.

Mackenzie Schubert Polonyi Donnelly

Mackenzie Polonyi is a Pushcart Prize-nominated Hungarian American poet and the author of *Post-Volcanic Folk Tales*, a winner of the National Poetry Series 2023, under contract with Akashic Books for publication in December 2024. Her work may be found or is forthcoming in *Barrelhouse Magazine*, *Crab Creek Review*, *Palette Poetry*, *Hayden's Ferry Review*, *Tupelo Press*, *Superstition Review*, *Diode Poetry Journal*, *Driftwood Press*, *Quarterly West*, where she was a finalist for their 2022 Poetry Contest, and elsewhere. She was A Public Space 2023 Writing Fellowship finalist. Mackenzie is a Cornell University 2022 MFA Poetry graduate, lecturer, and 2021 Robert Chasen Memorial Poetry Prize winner.

Rebecca A. Durham

Rebecca A. Durham is a poet, botanist, and artist. Originally from the Connecticut River Valley of New England, she also calls western Montana home. She earned a BA in Biology from Colby College, a MS in Botany from Oregon State University, an MFA in Creative Writing (Poetry) from the University of Montana, and a PhD in Interdisciplinary Studies from the University of Montana. For the last 13 years she has been researching vascular plants and lichens at the MPG Ranch, a conservation research property. Winner of the 2019 Many Voices in Poetry Contest, her debut poetry collection *Half-life of Empathy* was published by New Rivers Press in 2020. Loss/Less, her second poetry manuscript, was chosen by Susan Howe for the Marsh Hawk Press Rochelle Ratner Memorial Award and published by Shanti Arts in 2022. Find more of her work at rebeccadurham.net.

Karen Earle

Karen Earle is a private practice psychotherapist. She recently served as faculty member of the New Directions Program/Writing with a Psychoanalytic Edge. Before becoming a psychotherapist, she earned an MFA in Poetry from the University of Massachusetts, Amherst, was adjunct faculty at Widener University, and director of the writing lab at Bryn Mawr Graduate School of Social Work and Social Research. Her poetry has appeared in various journals, including the *G W Review*, *Chaffin Journal*, *Chaminade*, *Denver Quarterly Literary Review*, *Hudson Valley Echoes*, *Sugar House Review*, *Clade Song*, and *SWWIM*. She was a semifinalist in the Slapering Hol Chapbook Contest and was awarded a Martha's Vineyard Institute for Creative Writing fellowship. She has attended several Colrain Poetry Conferences to complete work on her manuscript *Honey & Sting*. She lives in Shelburne Falls, Massachusetts.

Kristina Erny

Kristina Erny is the author of *Elijah Fed by Ravens* (Solum Literary Press, 2023) and the chapbook *Put a Comma in Front of a Person* (2024), winner of the Harbor Review Editor's Prize. A third-culture poet who grew up in South Korea, she is always homesick for someone and somewhere. She holds an MFA from the University of Arizona, and her work has been the recipient of the Tupelo Quarterly Inaugural Poetry Prize and the Ruskin Art Club Poetry Award, as well as a finalist for the Coniston Prize. Her poems have appeared in *Southern Humanities Review*, *Los Angeles Review*, *Yemassee*, *Blackbird*, *Tupelo Quarterly*, *Rattle*, and elsewhere. She currently lives and works in Shanghai, China, with her family.

Gibson Fay-LeBlanc

Gibson Fay-LeBlanc's first collection of poems, *Death of a Ventriloquist*, won the Vassar Miller Prize and was featured by *Poets & Writers* as one of a dozen debut collections to watch. His second book, *Deke Dangle Dive*, was published by CavanKerry Press in 2021. Gibson's poems have appeared in magazines including the *New Republic*, *Tin House*, *Narrative*, *Poetry Northwest*, and *Orion*. With graduate degrees from the University of California, Berkeley, and Columbia University, Gibson has taught writing at conferences, schools, and universities including Fordham, Haystack, and University of Southern

Maine, and helped lead community arts organizations including the Telling Room, SPACE Gallery, and Hewnoaks Artist Colony. He currently serves as the Executive Director of the Maine Writers & Publishers Alliance and lives in Portland with his family.

Lisa Furmanski

Lisa Furmanski is a writer and physician living in New Hampshire. Her poetry has appeared in *Poetry*, *Antioch Review*, *Gettysburg Review*, *Prairie Schooner*, *Tupelo Quarterly*, *Hunger Mountain*, and elsewhere. Her chapbook, *Tunnel*, was published by Finishing Line Press in 2023 as part of the New Women's Voices series. She is the winner of the 2024 Marjorie Perkoff prize from the *Missouri Review*. Selected poems have been featured on Verse Daily and Poetry Daily. Her work can be found at lisafurmanski.com.

Deborah Gorlin

Deborah Gorlin is the author of two previous books of poems, *Bodily Course*, White Pine Poetry Press Prize, 1997, and *Life of the Garment*, winner of the 2014 May Sarton New Hampshire Poetry Prize. Her new book of poems, *Open Fire*, was published by Bauhan in spring 2023. Her work has appeared in a wide range of journals including *Poetry*, *American Poetry Review*, *Bomb*, *New England Review*, *Prairie Schooner*, and *Best Spiritual Writing 2000*. Recent poems have been published in *Plume*, *On the Seawall*, *Ekphrastic Review*, *Mass Poetry: The Hard Work of Hope*, *The Common*, *Rumors, Secrets & Lies*, *SWWIM*, and *Yetzirah*. Her lyric essay "Jack of All Trades" was a finalist in Calyx magazine's 2022 Margarita Donnelly Prize for Prose Writing. Emerita co-director of the Writing Program at Hampshire College, she served for many years as a poetry editor at *The Massachusetts Review*.

Jenny Grassl

Jenny Grassl is a poet and visual artist living in Cambridge, Massachusetts. She was raised in Collegeville, Pennsylvania. She received a BFA from Rhode Island School of Design in photography, and an MFA in poetry from Bennington Writing Seminars. She worked as a freelance artist and as a display designer for a retail store. Her current artwork includes digital collages and woodcuts. Her poems have appeared or are forthcoming in *Ocean State Review*, *Boston Review*, *Tupelo Quarterly*, *Bennington Review*, *Lana Turner Journal*, *Poetry International*, *Heavy Feather Review*, *Lit*, *Grolier Prize*, and others. Her poetry was featured in a Best of American Poetry blog. Her full-length poetry book, *Magicholia*, is forthcoming from 3: A Taos Press. The book will include images of some of her woodcuts.

Bonney Hartley

Bonney Hartley is a '25 MFA-Creative Writing candidate at the Institute of American Indian Arts in Santa Fe and holds an MSocSci in International Relations from the University of Cape Town, South Africa. She is an enrolled member of the Stockbridge-Munsee Community and serves as a repatriation specialist. She is a founding member of the Mohican Writers Circle. Her work has appeared in *Stonecoast Review*, the "Returning Home" exhibit (commission by Bard College), and *North Berkshire Landscapes: A Celebration* (Tupelo Press and Williamstown Rural Lands, 2024), and is forthcoming in *Boundless* (Mead Museum). Bonney is a 2024 Indigenous Nations Poetry Fellow. She lives within Mohican homelands in Williamstown, Massachusetts.

Rosemary Herbert

Rosemary Herbert's wide-ranging writings encompass poetry, journalism, reference works, and mystery and mainstream fiction. Her books include *The Oxford Companion to Crime & Mystery Writing*, *A New Omnibus of Crime*, *The Oxford Book of American Detective Stories*, and *Front Page Teaser: A Liz Higgins*

Mystery. She has worked on an archeological dig in Winchester, England; as a reference librarian at Harvard University; and as book review editor and garden columnist at the *Boston Herald*. She has reviewed for the *New York Times Book Review*, *Washington Post*, and *Minneapolis Star-Tribune*, and contributed interviews to the *Paris Review* and *Harvard Review*. Her poetry appears in *Radar Poetry*, *Beyond Words Literary Magazine*, and in *Tiny Seed Literary Journal* and their *Poetry of the Wild Flowers* anthology. She received first prize in the Dreamers 2024 Haiku Contest. She resides in Akron, Ohio, where she also pursues ceramic arts, specializing in creating mosaics and porcelain sewing buttons.

Rick Hilles

Rick Hilles is the author of *Brother Salvage*, selected by Kim Addonizio as the winner of the 2005 Agnes Lynch Starrett Prize (and named 2006 Poetry Book of the Year by *ForeWord* magazine), and *A Map of the Lost World*, a finalist for the 2012 Ohioana Poetry Prize. His most recent poetry collection is *My Roberto Clemente* (C&R Press, 2021). A recipient of the Amy Lowell Traveling Poetry Scholarship, a Fulbright, and a Whiting Writers Award, his poems, essays, and translations have appeared or are forthcoming in *American Literary Review*, *Black Warrior Review*, *Harper's*, *Kenyon Review*, *Literary Imagination*, *Missouri Review*, *Narrative*, the *Nation*, *New Letters*, the *New Republic*, *Paris Review*, *Poetry*, *Ploughshares*, *Provincetown Arts*, *Salmagundi*, and *Southern Review*. He teaches in the English Department and MFA program at Vanderbilt University and lives in Nashville, Tennessee, and Carrboro, North Carolina.

Eva Hooker

In my first book, *Godwit* (3: A Taos Press 2916), I traced the migration patterns of a bird, collected wildflowers for semblances, and rooted around in the testimony of women mystics. I like to wander in places strange to me. I like to explore without linguistic obligation. My second manuscript, *Portion*, leans up out of the shade and explores the compass of the world in

Margaret Cavendish's 17th-century voice. My poems have been published in journals such as *Agni*, *Notre Dame Review*, *Salmagundi*, *Orion*, *Salamander*, and *Presences*. I am professor of English and writer in residence at Saint Mary's College, Notre Dame, Indiana.

Luisa A. Igloria

Luisa A. Igloria is the author of *Caulbearer* (Immigrant Writing Series Prize, Black Lawrence Press, 2024), *Maps for Migrants and Ghosts* (2020), *The Buddha Wonders if She is Having a Mid-Life Crisis* (2018), 12 other books, and four chapbooks. She is lead editor, with co-editors Aileen Cassinetto and Jeremy S. Hoffman, of *Dear Human at the Edge of Time: Poems on Climate Change in the U.S.* (Paloma Press, 2023), offered as a companion to the Fifth National Climate Assessment (NCA5). Originally from Baguio City, she is the Louis I. Jaffe and University Professor of English and Creative Writing at Old Dominion University's MFA Creative Writing Program. She also leads workshops for and is a member of the board of the Muse Writers Center in Norfolk. Luisa is the twentieth Poet Laureate of the Commonwealth of Virginia (2020–22), emerita. During her term, the Academy of American Poets awarded her a 2021 Poet Laureate Fellowship. www.luisaigloria.com.

Didi Jackson

Didi Jackson is the author of *Moon Jar* and the forthcoming collection *My Infinity*. Her poems have appeared in *American Poetry Review*, *Kenyon Review*, the *New Yorker*, *Oxford American*, and *World Literature Today*, among other journals and magazines. She has had poems selected for *Best American Poetry*, *Academy of American Poets' Poem-a-day*, and *The Slow Down* with Tracy K. Smith. She is the recipient of the Robert H. Winner Memorial Award from the Poetry Society of America and was a finalist for the Meringoff Prize in Poetry. She lives in Nashville, Tennessee, where she teaches creative writing at Vanderbilt University.

John James

John James is the author of *The Milk Hours* (Milkweed, 2019), selected by Henri Cole for the Max Ritvo Poetry Prize, as well as three chapbooks, most recently *Extinction Song* (Tupelo, 2026), winner of the Snowbound Chapbook Award. His poems appear in *Boston Review*, *Kenyon Review*, *Gulf Coast*, *PEN Poetry Series*, *Best American Poetry*, and elsewhere. His work has been supported by fellowships and awards from the Bread Loaf Environmental Writers Conference, the Academy of American Poets, and the Lannan Center for Poetics and Social Practice at Georgetown University. He holds an MFA in poetry from Columbia and is completing a PhD in English at the University of California, Berkeley.

s. d. lishan

s. d. lishan's book of poetry, *Body Tapestries* (Dream Horse Press), was awarded the Orphic Prize in Poetry. Their poetry, fiction, and creative nonfiction have appeared in *Measure*, *Phoebe*, *Arts & Letters*, *Kenyon Review*, *Cutbank*, *Creative Nonfiction*, and many other journals that feature passion and solace for the sweet words. They live and write in Columbus, Ohio, where they teach at the Ohio State University.

Katherine Cota MacDonald

Katherine Cota MacDonald (she/her) resides in Massachusetts. She began writing poetry in her youth and has ushered life's transitions into her work. Themes of nature, parenting, joy, mental health, and the tide of the creative spirit line her works. Katherine is an artist and educator and she runs her own small business, Rosewood Bloc, providing wellness and mindfulness programming. She received her BA in Psychology from the University of Massachusetts, Lowell, and is currently pursuing her MSW.

Sarah Maclay

Sarah Maclay is the author of five collections of poetry—most recently, *Nightfall Marginalia* (What Books Press), a 2023 Foreword INDIES Finalist—and three chapbooks, as well as the forthcoming *The HD Sequence: A Concordance*, her fourth. Published widely, her work has been supported and honored by a Yaddo residency, a City of Los Angeles Individual Artist Fellowship, the Tampa Review Prize for Poetry, and a Pushcart Special Mention, appearing in *APR, FIELD, Ploughshares, Tupelo Quarterly, Writer's Chronicle, The Best American Erotic Poetry: From 1800 to the Present, Poetry International*, where she served as book review editor for a decade, and elsewhere, as well as providing the lyrical basis for a series of classical art songs, composed by Kostas Rekleitis, available on the album *Identity Had Gone*. She has taught creative writing and literature at Loyola Marymount University for nearly two decades and offers periodic workshops at Beyond Baroque in Venice, California.

Marjorie Maddox

Professor Emeritus of Commonwealth University, Marjorie Maddox has published 16 collections of poetry—including *Transplant, Transport, Transubstantiation* (Yellowglen Prize), *Begin with a Question* (International Book and Illumination Book Award Winners), the Shanti Arts ekphrastic collaborations *Heart Speaks, Is Spoken For* (with photographer Karen Elias), *In the Museum of My Daughter's Mind*, a collaboration with her artist daughter, Anna Lee Hafer (www.hafer.work), and others. Her newest books are *How Can I Look It Up When I Don't Know How It's Spelled? Spelling Mnemonics and Grammar Tricks* (Kelsay, 2024) and *Seeing Things* (Wildhouse, 2024). In addition, she has published the story collection *What She Was Saying* (Fomite) and four children's books. With Jerry Wemple, she is co-editor of *Common Wealth: Contemporary Poets on Pennsylvania* and the forthcoming *Keystone Poetry: Contemporary Poets on Pennsylvania* (PSU Press). She is assistant editor of *Presence* and hosts WPSU's Poetry Moment. Please see www.marjoriemaddox.com.

Libby Maxey

Libby Maxey is a senior editor and poetry editor at *Literary Mama*. Her work has appeared in *Crannóg*, *The Maynard*, and elsewhere. She is a winner of the Princemere Poetry Prize and the Helen Schaible International Sonnet Contest, and her chapbook *Kairos* (2019) won Finishing Line Press's New Women's Voices contest. Her nonliterary activities include singing classical repertoire and mothering sons.

Susan McCabe

Susan McCabe is a professor at the University of Southern California in Los Angeles, teaching poetics, modernism, ecology, and creative writing. She is a past president of the Modernist Studies Association. She has received a Fulbright, a residential fellowship at American Academy in Berlin, as well as a fellowship at Stanford's Humanities Center in 2016. She has published two books of poetry, one a Lambda Literary finalist, Swirl, the other her award-winning *Descartes' Nightmare* (University of Utah Press, 2008), and two critical books, *Elizabeth Bishop: Her Poetics of Loss*, and *Cinematic Modernism*. Most recently, she has published a dual bi-biography, *H. D & Bryher: An Untold Love Story of Modernism* (Oxford, November 2021). She has directed the PhD program in Creative Writing at USC, and her manuscript *I Woke a Lake* will be published in 2025. Along with many essays and introductions, her poetry reviews have appeared recently in *Los Angeles Review of Books* and *Denver Quarterly*, among other venues.

James McCorkle

James McCorkle's collections of poems include *Evidences* (2003 recipient of the APR-Honickman First Book Award), *The Subtle Bodies* (Etruscan Press 2014), and *In Time* (Etruscan Press, 2020). His poems have appeared in or are forthcoming from *APR*, *Bennington Review*, *Chant de la Sirene*, *Conjunctions*, *Harvard Review*,

Kenyon Review, *Poetry*, *Raritan*, and many others. He has been a recipient of an NEA Fellowship and an Ingram Merrill grant. He co-directs the Africana Studies Program at Hobart and William Smith Colleges in Geneva, New York.

Becka Mara McKay

Becka Mara McKay is a poet and a translator of Hebrew literature. She directs the Creative Writing MFA at Florida Atlantic University, where she serves as faculty advisor to *Swamp Ape Review*. Her newest book of poems is *The Little Book of No Consolation* (Barrow Street Press).

Alicia Rebecca Myers

Alicia Rebecca Myers is a poet and essayist who holds an MFA in Poetry from New York University. Her writing has appeared in publications that include *Best New Poets*, *Creative Nonfiction*, *River Styx*, *FIELD*, *Gulf Coast*, *SWWIM*, *december*, *Sixth Finch*, and *The Rumpus*. Her chapbook of poems, *My Seaborgium* (Brain Mill Press, 2016), was winner of the Mineral Point Chapbook Series. Her first full-length book, *Warble*, was chosen by former Kansas Poet Laureate Caryn Mirriam-Goldberg as winner of the 2024 Birdy Poetry Prize and will be published in spring 2025 (Meadowlark Press). She lives with her husband and nine-year-old son in upstate New York.

William Orem

William Orem's first collection of stories, *Zombi, You My Love*, won the GLCA New Writers Award, formerly given to Louise Erdrich, Sherman Alexie, Richard Ford, and Alice Munro. His second collection, *Across the River*, won the Texas Review Novella Prize. His first novel, *Killer of Crying Deer*, won the Eric Hoffer Award and has been optioned for film. His first collection of poems, *Our Purpose in Speaking*, won the Wheelbarrow Books Poetry Prize. It also won the Rubery International Book Award in poetry and was chosen book of the year. His second novel, *Miss Lucy*, won the Gival Press

Novel Award; *Kirkus* listed it as one of the Best Books of 2019. He has been nominated for the Pushcart Prize five times, in poetry, fiction, and creative nonfiction. Meanwhile, his short plays have been performed internationally, winning both the Critics' Prize and Audience Favorite Award at Durango Theatre Fest, and thrice being nominated for the prestigious Heideman Award at Actors Theatre of Louisville (Kentucky). Currently he is a Senior Writer-in-Residence at Emerson College. williamorem.com.

Preeti Parikh

Preeti Parikh is a poet and essayist with a past educational background in medicine and a recent MFA from the Rainier Writing Workshop. Her writing appears in *Beloit Poetry Journal*, *Cincinnati Review*, *The Margins*, and other literary journals and anthologies. A Kundiman Fellow and recipient of grant awards from the Sustainable Arts Foundation and the Ohio Arts Council, Preeti has received support for her work from Millay Arts, Bread Loaf Writers' Conference, AWP Writer to Writer Program, and Tin House Winter Workshop. Born and raised in India, she now lives with her family in a multigenerational home in Ohio. preetiparikh.com.

Elise Paschen

Elise Paschen's next book of poetry, *Blood Wolf Moon*, will be published in 2025. An enrolled member of the Osage Nation, she is the author of six poetry collections, most recently, *Tallchief*. As an undergraduate at Harvard, she received the Garrison Medal for poetry. She holds MPhil and DPhil degrees from Oxford University. Her poems have been published widely, including in *Poetry*, the *New Yorker*, *A Norton Anthology of Native Nations Poetry*, and *The Best American Poetry*. She has edited or co-edited numerous anthologies, including *The Eloquent Poem* and the *New York Times* bestseller, *Poetry Speaks*. Paschen teaches in the MFA Writing Program at the School of the Art Institute of Chicago.

Veronica Patterson

Veronica Patterson's poetry collections include *How to Make a Terrarium* (CSU Poetry Center, 1987), *Swan, What Shores?* (NYU Press Poetry Prize, 2000), *Thresh & Hold* (Gell Poetry Prize, 2009), *& it had rained* (CW Books, 2013), and *Sudden White Fan* (Cherry Grove, 2018), and two chapbooks, *This Is the Strange Part* (2002) and *Maneuvers: Battle of the Little Bighorn Poems* (2013). Her poems "Around the Block of the World" and "The Samovar" co-won the 2006 Campbell Corner Poetry Prize. Honors include Pushcart nominations, Writer's Almanac, Verse Daily publications, and two individual Colorado Council on the Arts grants. Patterson graduated from Cornell University (Phi Beta Kappa), University of Michigan, University of Northern Colorado, and Warren Wilson (MFA Poetry). Her *Georgia Review* (Spring 1993) essay, "Comfort Me with Apples," was selected as a Notable Essay of the Year. She was Loveland, Colorado's, first Poet Laureate, serving from 2019 through 2022.

Martha Ronk

Martha Ronk is the author of 13 books of poetry, most recently *The Place One Is* (Omnidawn 2022) and *A Myth of Ariadne*, influenced by De Chirico's paintings of Ariadne (Parlor Press 2022). *Transfer of Qualities* was long-listed for the National Book Award, and *Vertigo* was a National Poetry Series selection. She attended both Djerassi and MacDowell and received an NEA grant. Her academic career was as Professor of English at Occidental College in Los Angeles.

Steven Salmoni

Steven Salmoni's recent publications include *A Day of Glass* and the chapbook *Landscape, With Green Mangoes* (both from Chax Press), and poems in *Puerto del Sol*, *P-Queue*, *Mid-American Review*, *Brooklyn Review*, and *Interim*. Selections from his work have also appeared in the anthologies *The Experiment Will Not Be Bound* (Unbound Editions, 2022), *The Sonoran Desert: A Literary Field Guide*

(University of Arizona Press, 2016), and *The Salt Companion to Charles Bernstein* (Salt Publishing, 2012). He received a PhD from Stony Brook University and is currently the department chair of English at Pima Community College in Tucson, Arizona. He also serves on the board of directors for Chax Press and for POG, a Tucson-based literary and arts organization that hosts an annual reading series.

Mara Adamitz Scrupe

Mara Adamitz Scrupe is a poet, visual artist, and documentary filmmaker. Her publications include five full poetry collections, selections in generational anthologies by *Southword*/Munster Literature, *Aesthetica*, *Stony Thursday*, and *64 Best Poets*/Black Mountain Press, and poems in key international journals including *Radar*, *Rhino*, *Tupelo Quarterly*, *Cincinnati Review*, *London Magazine*, *Mslexia*, *Magma*, *Abridged*, and *The Poetry Business/ Smith Doorstop*. Twice nominated for the Pushcart Prize in Poetry, she has won or been short-listed for significant literary awards including Arts University Bournemouth International Poetry Prize, Magma Pamphlet Publication Award, Gregory O'Donohugh International Poetry Prize, Pablo Neruda Poetry Prize, and National Poetry Society UK. Mara is a MacDowell Fellow, and she serves concurrently as Distinguished Visiting Professor in the Liberal Arts, University of Minnesota Morris, and Dean and Professor Emerita, University of the Arts Philadelphia. She resides with her husband on their farm in the Blue Ridge Piedmont countryside of Virginia.

Annette Sisson

Annette Sisson's poems have appeared in *Valparaiso Poetry Review*, *Birmingham Poetry Review*, *Rust and Moth*, *Lascaux Review*, *Glassworks*, *Sky Island Journal*, *Blue Mountain Review*, *Five South*, *Cider Press Review*, *West Trade Review*, and many other journals and anthologies. Her first full-length book, *Small Fish in High Branches*, was published by Glass Lyre (2022), and her second, *Winter*

Sharp with Apples, will be published by Terrapin Books in October 2024. She was named a Mark Strand Poetry Scholar for the 2021 Sewanee Writers' Conference and a 2020 BOAAT Writing Fellow. Her poem "Fog" won the Porch Writers' Collective's 2019 poetry prize, and her poems have placed in several contests, including Frontier New Voices and the Fish Anthology. She has received multiple nominations for the Pushcart Prize and Best of the Net, three of which occurred in 2023. http://annettesisson.com.

Arthur Solway

Arthur Solway is the author of two collections of poetry, *Siddhartha On Fire* (Swan Scythe Press) and *Friday Night, Shanghai* (Finishing Line Press). His poetry, essays, and reviews have appeared in *Antioch Review*, *Artforum*, *Arts & Letters*, *ArtAsiaPacific*, *Barrow Street*, *BOMB*, *Frieze*, *London Magazine*, *Salmagundi*, *Southern Poetry Review*, *TriQuarterly*, and *Tupelo Quarterly*, and have been featured by the Academy of American Poets' Poem-a-Day. Living as an expatriate in Shanghai for well over a decade, he was the founding director of the first contemporary art gallery from New York to establish itself in mainland China. He presently lives in Santa Cruz, California.

L. Stuart

L. Stuart is a novelist, essayist, and poet who lives and writes in the Midwest.

Natalie Taylor

Natalie Taylor leads a writerly life and relishes poeming in her garden. She earned a BFA in English with a creative writing emphasis from the University of Utah. She is the author of the poetry chapbook *Eden's Edge*, from Finishing Line Press, and her work has been published in *15 Bytes*, *Hubbub*, *Hunger Mountain*, *Kettle Blue Review*, *New Ohio Review*, *Rock & Sling*, *SWWIM Every Day*, and *Talking River*. She won first place in the 2016 Utah Original Writing competition and second place in the 2023 Utah Original Writing competition, both for poetry, and was named a 2017 Mari Sandoz Emerging Writer: Poetry.

G. C. Waldrep

G. C. Waldrep's most recent books are *feast gently* (Tupelo, 2018), winner of the William Carlos Williams Award from the Poetry Society of America, *The Earliest Witnesses* (Tupelo/Carcanet, 2021), and *The Opening Ritual* (Tupelo, forthcoming 2024). Recent work has appeared in *American Poetry Review*, *Poetry*, *Paris Review*, *Ploughshares*, *New England Review*, *Yale Review*, the *Nation*, *New American Writing*, *Conjunctions*, and other journals. Waldrep lives in Lewisburg, Pennsylvania, where he teaches at Bucknell University.

Calleja Smiley Welsh

Calleja Smiley Welsh is a poet and dancer. She is the inaugural winner of the Richard Howard Memorial Prize in Poetry, and is currently an MFA candidate in Poetry and a University Writing Instructor at Columbia University. She holds a BFA in Dance Performance from Dominican University of California/LINES Ballet, and her dance career has included performing with the Merce Cunningham Trust and working as a Community Actionist with Gibney. Calleja's poetry has been published in *No, Dear* magazine, and her original moving-poem solos—simultaneous performances of dance and spoken text—have been presented through Judson Church in New York City and the Cleveland Dance Fest. She began writing poems as a way to choreograph the space and time of an empty page and continues to do so because she always has one more poem to write about plants. Calleja lives with her husband in Manhattan.

Laura Budofsky Wisniewski

Laura Budofsky Wisniewski is the author of *Sanctuary, Vermont* (Orison Books), which won the 2020 Orison Poetry Prize, the New England Poetry Club's 2022 Sheila Margaret Motton Book Prize, and the 2022 Bronze Foreword INDIES Poetry Book of the Year Award. She is also author of the chapbook *How to Prepare Bear* (Redbird Chapbooks). She was a finalist in the 2022 Narrative Poetry Prize, runner-up in the 2021 *Missouri Review* Miller Audio Prize, and winner of *Ruminate* magazine's 2020 Janet B. McCabe Poetry Prize, the 2019 Poetry International Prize, and the 2014 Passager Poetry Prize. Her work has appeared in *On the Seawall*, *Poetry International*, *Narrative*, *Missouri Review*, *Chicago Quarterly Review*, *Image*, and other journals. Laura lives quietly in a small town in Vermont.

EDITORS

Alan Berolzheimer

Alan Berolzheimer is a consulting editor for Tupelo Press with over forty years of experience in the world of publishing.

Jeffrey Levine

Jeffrey is the author of three books of poetry: *At the Kinnegad Home for the Bewildered* (Salmon Poetry, 2019), *Rumor of Cortez*, nominated for a 2006 Los Angeles Times Literary Award in Poetry, and *Mortal, Everlasting*, which won the 2002 Transcontinental Poetry Prize. His many poetry prizes include the Larry Levis Prize from the *Missouri Review*, the James Hearst Poetry Prize from *North American Review*, the *Mississippi Review* Poetry Prize, the *Ekphrasis* Poetry Prize, and the *American Literary Review* poetry prize. His poems have garnered 21 Pushcart nominations. A graduate of the Warren Wilson MFA Program for Writers, Levine is founder, artistic director, and publisher of Tupelo Press, an award-winning independent literary press located in the historic NORAD Mill in the Berkshire Mountains of Western Massachusetts.

Allison O'Keefe

Allison O'Keefe is an operations administrator and book designer at Tupelo Press. She is a graduate of Massachusetts College of Liberal Arts, and she lives in North Adams, Massachusetts.